HOW TO GROW

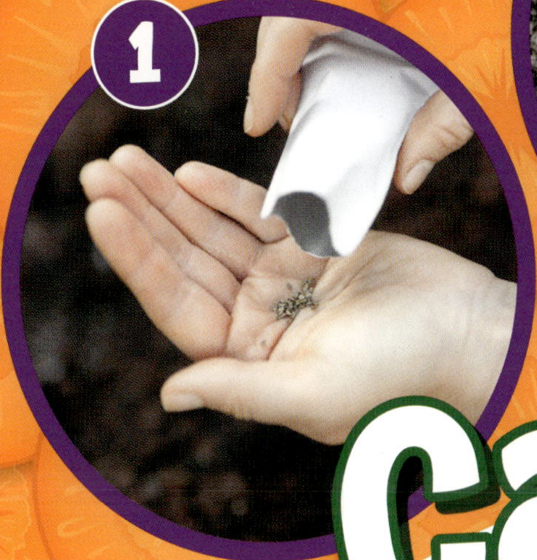

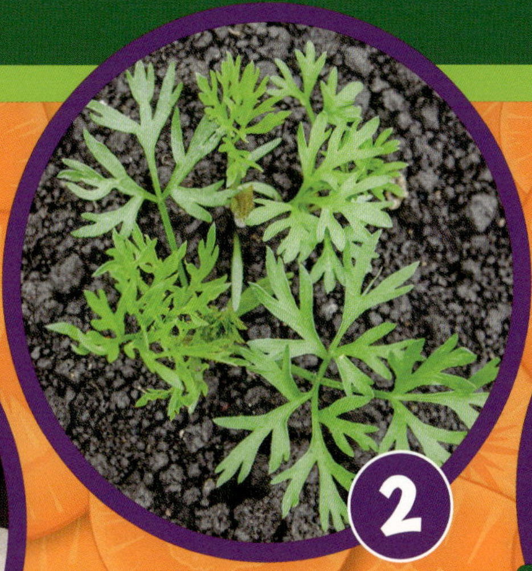

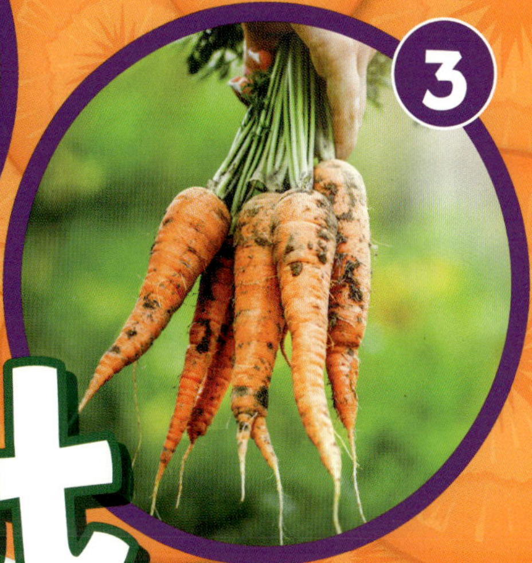

1

2

3

Carrot Cake

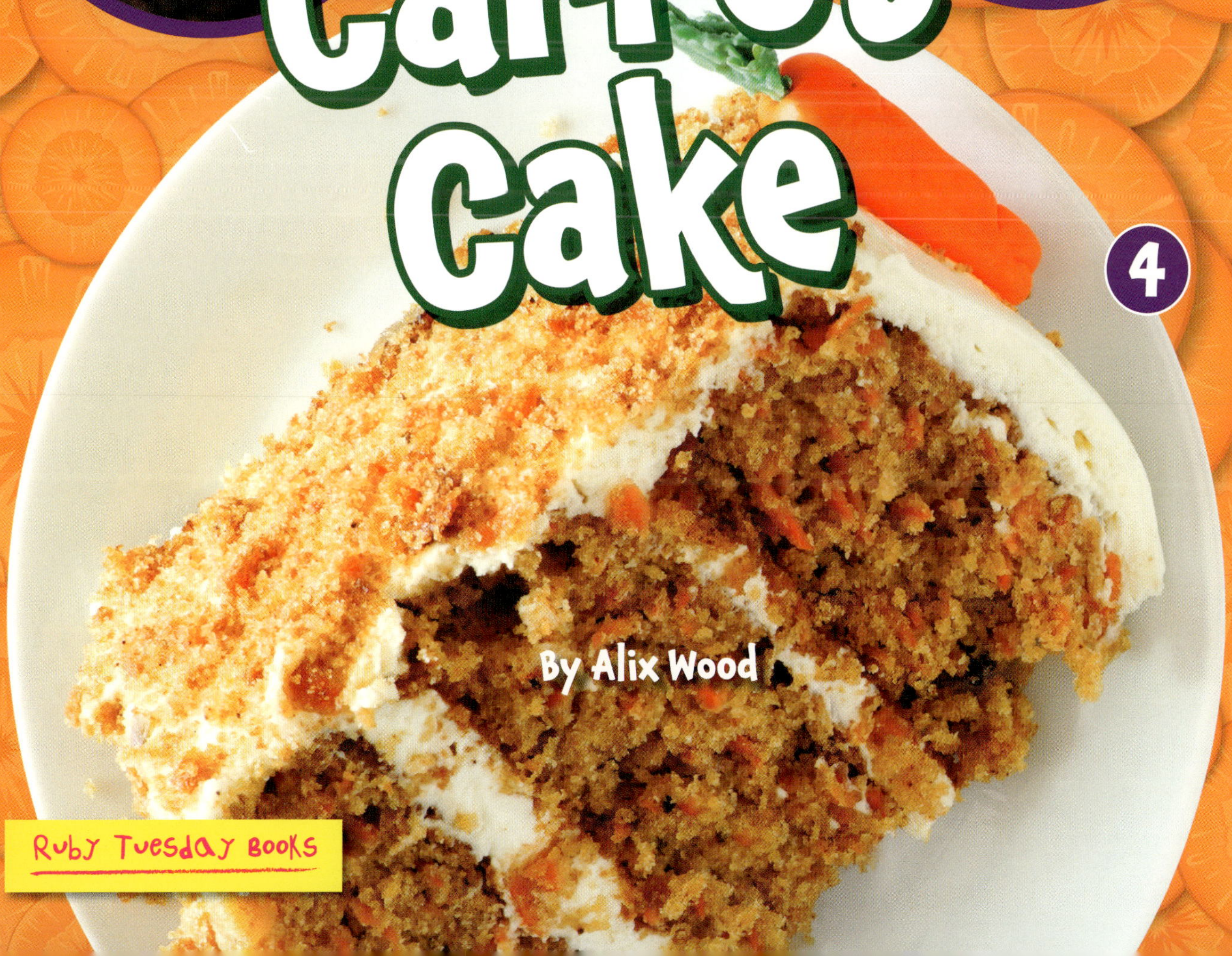

4

By Alix Wood

Ruby Tuesday Books

Published in 2024 by Ruby Tuesday Books Ltd.

Copyright © 2024 Ruby Tuesday Books Ltd.

Editor: Ruth Owen & Mark J. Sachner
Design: Alix Wood
Production: John Lingham

Photo credits:
Alamy: 10B (Dorling Kindersley); Ruby Tuesday Books: 7, 15B, 18B, 19, 20; Shutterstock: Cover (JeniFoto/Max_555/Janna Markina/Krasula/Ansty), 4 (MaraZe/New Africa/Spalnic/Enlightened Media), 5 (bigacis/Nataliia Budianska/Hong Vo/baibaz), 6 (Casther), 7 (Becky Starsmore/Nattika), 8 (Igor Zoiko/HelloSSTK/Hortimages/bergamont), 9 (GreenThumbShots/Diana Taliun/cameilia/Ilina93/FabrikaSimf/New Africa/Vitawin), 10T (Diyana Dimitrova), 11, 12B (Janna Markina), 13T (Michele Ursi/Tomasz Klejdysz), 13B (Zerbor), 14T (Andrii Bezvershenko), 14C (Nataly Studio), 14B (koosen), 15T (jaap posthumus), 16T (Olga Ilinich), 16C (Cohncentric), 16B (garmoncheg), 17 (wk1003mike/Leka Sergeeva/Dobra Kobra), 18T (Irina Simkina), 19, 20 (vm2002), 21 (Maren Winter/Jemma Craig/Moving Moment/krutar), 22 (Natasha Breen/Anzhela Shvab/ch123), 23 (stuar/Shy Radar/casther); Alix Wood: 11, 12T.

Library of Congress Control Number: 2023952372

Print (Hardback) ISBN 978-1-78856-349-9
Print (Paperback) ISBN 978-1-78856-350-5
ePub ISBN 978-1-78856-352-9

Published in Minneapolis, MN
Printed in the United States

www.rubytuesdaybooks.com

Contents

A Superhero Food

Do you like to munch on a crunchy, raw carrot? You can also eat carrots steamed, mashed, and roasted. You can grate them and add them to a salad. Or you can even turn them into yummy

CARROT CAKE.

Carrots are full of **beta-carotene**. This substance gives some fruits and vegetables their bright colors.

Carrots are good for us. Our bodies turn the beta-carotene into **vitamin A**.

Vitamin A is good for our eyes, bones, teeth, and skin.

In the past, the best cheddar cheese was made from cows that ate grass full of beta-carotene. The substance made their milk and the cheese look a little orange. Cheesemakers who did not have this high-quality milk used carrots to dye their cheese orange.

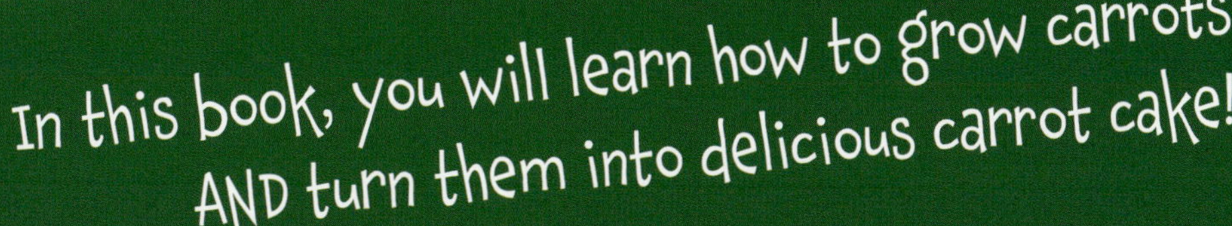

Roots and Leaves

Carrots are called **root** vegetables. That's because we eat the root of the plant.

A carrot plant has a long, thick root that grows straight down into the ground. It is called a **taproot**.

Carrot leaves are tasty and good for you, too.
You can actually grow carrot leaves from a carrot top!

- A carrot
- A knife and chopping board
- A shallow dish
- Water

BE SAFE!

Be sure that an adult is there to help you when you use a knife.

1 Carefully cut the top 1 inch (2.5 cm) off the carrot.

2 Place the carrot top in a shallow dish, cut side down.

3 Pour water into the dish so it covers the base of the carrot top.

4 Check the water every day. Add more if needed. After a few days, leaves will start to grow from the carrot top.

The carrot top will grow leaves and thin roots, but it will not grow a new taproot.

Chopped carrot leaves can be sprinkled on salads or soup. You can also stir them into plain yogurt to make a salad dressing or dip.

Get Ready to Grow!

Spring and summer are the best times for growing carrots. Many gardeners grow carrots in soil in a vegetable patch. But you can also grow carrots in a large container.

YOU WILL NEED:

- A packet of carrot seeds
- A container that's about 1.5 feet (46 cm) deep
- Pebbles: enough to cover the bottom of the container 1 inch (2.5 cm) deep
- A bag of potting soil
- Scissors
- A small garden trowel and fork
- A watering can

vegetable patch

Carrot plants

1 Buy a packet of carrot **seeds** from a store or online.

The store will probably have different types of carrot seeds for sale. If your container is deep, choose seeds that grow into long carrots. If it's not very deep, try growing shorter, rounder carrots.

2 Make sure your container has at least one drainage hole in the bottom. If a plastic pot has no drainage holes, ask an adult to make some for you.

3 Cover the bottom of the pot with a layer of pebbles about 1 inch (2.5 cm) deep.

4 Using scissors, carefully cut open the bag of potting soil. Then use a garden trowel to fill the pot with soil almost to the top.

Sow Your Seeds

When your container is ready, it's time to sow, or plant, your seeds.

Carrot seeds

1 Using a trowel, scrape lines in the soil that are 0.5 inches (1.25 cm) deep. The lines should be 3 inches (7.5 cm) apart.

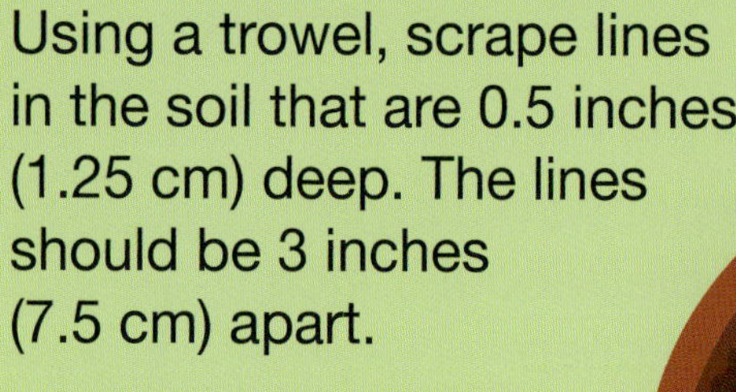

If you prefer, you can make circles in the soil that are 3 inches (7.5 cm) apart.

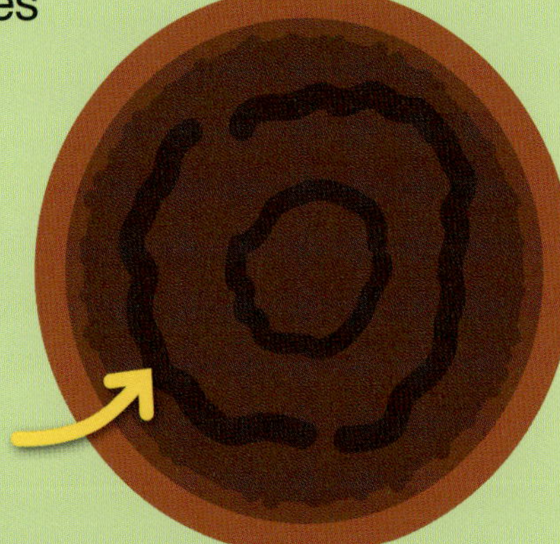

2 Sow your seeds thinly into the lines. The seeds should be about 1 inch (2.5 cm) apart.

Pinch some carrot seeds between your thumb and forefinger. Then roll your fingers back and forth, moving along the line. The seeds will drop into the soil about the right distance apart.

Now, you have to be patient! It will take up to three weeks for tiny **seedlings** to start appearing.

Caring for Your Plants

Seeds need warmth and water to grow. The Sun will give them heat. Rain or your watering can will give them water.

1 Check the soil in the container with your fingers every other day. If it feels dry, carefully water the soil until it feels moist.

2 After about three weeks, tiny green seedlings will grow up from the soil. Keep checking to see if they need water.

3 As your seedlings grow, other unwanted plants known as **weeds** may grow, too. Carefully pull any weeds from the soil.

Weeds might take water from your seedlings and keep them from getting enough sunshine and fresh air.

Carrot plant seedling

Your carrot plants also have an insect enemy—carrot flies.

Carrot fly

Carrot flies lay their eggs in the soil near carrot roots. When the flies' larvae hatch, they eat the carrot roots!

4 Be careful not to crush or damage your carrot plants' leaves when you are pulling weeds. The smell of carrot leaves attracts the flies.

Carrot fly larva

Damaged carrot root

5 Try growing another plant with a strong smell next to your carrots. The smell may confuse the flies and keep them from smelling your carrots.

Place a pot of mint next to the carrots.

Sow the seeds of quick-growing chives or scallions (green onions) around the edge of your container. Sow these seeds when you sow your carrots.

Carrot Science!

As a carrot plant's leaves grow upward, the orange taproot grows downward.

The leaves use sunlight to make sugary food for the growing plant.

The inner part of the orange carrot root is called the **xylem** (ZY-luhm). It takes water from the soil and moves it upward to the leaves.

Around the xylem is a part called the **phloem** (FLOW-em). It contains the sweet sugary food made by the leaves.

A carrot's phloem tastes sweeter than the xylem.

1 Keep carefully weeding the soil and watering your carrot plants.

2 As the orange carrot roots grow, check to see that they are not appearing above the soil. If they are, cover them with a little more soil.

Green carrot root

3 Check your plants for a spotty disease called leaf blight. It attacks a carrot plant's leaves in damp weather.

4 Carefully cut off any damaged leaves and throw them away. Then, when watering, be careful to only wet the soil and keep the plants' leaves as dry as possible.

Harvesting Your Crop

When carrots grow in the ground, they sometimes meet up with stones as they grow downward. This can make them grow in very funny shapes!

A carrot may change direction to avoid a stone.

It may grow in two directions.

Carrots that grow too close together may even wrap themselves around each other!

After about 12 to 16 weeks, your carrots will be ready to harvest.

1 Water the soil before you try to pull your carrots from the container. This helps soften the soil.

2 Next, carefully loosen the soil around the carrots with a small garden fork. Don't dig too close to the carrots or you might damage them.

3 Take hold of a carrot firmly near the base of the leaves and pull upward.

Garden fork

You don't have to harvest all your carrots at once. Just pull up as many as you need.

4 If you wish, you can leave three or four carrots in the container through the winter. In spring, your carrot plants will grow umbrella-like flowers.

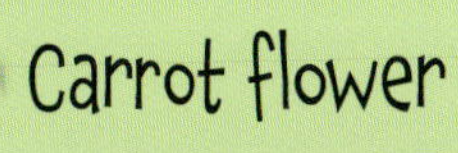

Carrot flower

In summer, the flowers will produce seeds. Wait until the flowers and seeds are dry. Then you can collect the seeds and use them to grow more carrots next year!

Let's Make Carrot Cake!

Equipment
- Measuring cups and spoons
- A grater
- Paper towel
- 2 9-inch (22-cm)-wide round cake pans
- Parchment paper
- 3 mixing bowls
- A wooden spoon
- An electric whisk or hand whisk
- Oven mitts
- 2 potholders or a hot pad
- A toothpick
- A cooling rack
- A rubber spatula

Cake Ingredients
- 2 cups (240 g) all-purpose flour
- 2 teaspoons baking soda
- ½ teaspoon salt
- 1 ½ teaspoons ground cinnamon
- 1 ¼ cups (295 ml) vegetable oil plus 1 tablespoon for greasing the pans
- 1 cup (200 g) granulated sugar
- 1 cup (190 g) light brown sugar
- 1 teaspoon vanilla extract
- 4 large eggs
- 3 cups (400 g) peeled and grated carrot
- 1 cup (200 g) chopped pecan nuts
- ½ cup (65 g) raisins

Frosting and Decoration Ingredients
- 1 stick (113 g) butter
- 1 cup (130 g) powdered sugar
- 8 ounces (225 g) cream cheese
- ½ cup (100 g) pecan nuts

You can use your homegrown carrots to make this delicious, sweet carrot cake.

1 Preheat the oven to 350°F (175°C).

2 Using a paper towel or your fingers, grease the cake pans with a little oil. Then line the pans with parchment paper.

3 In a bowl, mix together the flour, baking soda, salt, and cinnamon with a wooden spoon.

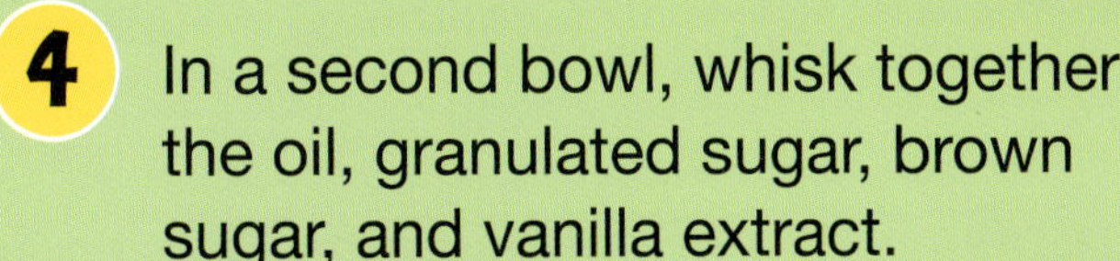

4 In a second bowl, whisk together the oil, granulated sugar, brown sugar, and vanilla extract.

5 One at a time, whisk the eggs into the oil mixture.

6 Next, add one-third of the flour mixture to the oil mixture. Stir with a wooden spoon. Add another third and stir. Add the final third and stir until the cake batter is smooth.

7 Finally, stir in the grated carrot, chopped pecans, and raisins.

8 Pour half of the cake batter into each cake pan.

9 Wearing oven mitts, carefully put the cakes into the center of the oven. Bake for 45 to 55 minutes.

10 Wearing oven mitts, remove the cakes from the oven and place on a hot pad or potholders.

BE SAFE!

Be sure that an adult is there to help you when you are using the oven.

The top of the cakes should feel springy.

You can test if a cake is baked by inserting a toothpick into the center. If the toothpick comes out clean, it is ready.

11 Let the cakes cool for 15 minutes. Then take hold of the parchment paper and lift each cake from its pan onto a cooling rack. Allow to cool completely and then peel off the paper.

12 To make the frosting, put the butter and powdered sugar into the bowl. Whisk together until smooth and fluffy.

13 Next, whisk in the cream cheese, a little at a time.

14 Using a rubber spatula, spread half the frosting on top of one of the cakes. Then place the second cake on top.

15 Spread the rest of the frosting over the top of the cake. Decorate with pecans.

Keep on pulling and eating your carrots, and enjoy your homegrown carrot cake!

Glossary

beta-carotene
A colorful substance that gives some plants, fruits, and vegetables their bright colors. It is found in carrots, tomatoes, peppers, and squash.

larvae
The young of some insects, such as flies and beetles.

moist
Slightly wet.

phloem
The part of a plant that carries sugary food from the leaves to other parts of the plant.

root
An underground part of a plant. Roots take in water and helpful substances called nutrients from the soil.

seed
A tiny part of a plant that contains all the material needed to grow a new plant.

seedling

A small, new plant that is growing from a seed.

taproot

A single large, thick root that grows down into the soil. Small, thin roots grow from the taproot.

vitamin A

A substance found in foods such as vegetables, fish, milk, and eggs that is very good for us.

weed

A wild plant that is growing where it is not wanted. Weeds are tough and usually grow quickly.

xylem

The part of a plant that carries water from the roots up to the leaves and other parts of the plant.

Index

Read More

Owen, Ruth. *Fruits and Vegetables: How We Grow and Eat Them (Get Started With STEM)*. Minneapolis, MN: Ruby Tuesday Books (2022).

Wood, Alix. *How to Grow Potato Chips.* Minneapolis, MN: Ruby Tuesday Books (2024).